M000104864

Best

BIG

Joke Book
for Kids

Peter MacDonald

Copyright © 2017 Peter MacDonald

All rights reserved.

ISBN-13: 978-0-9954362-1-3
ISBN-10: 0-9954362-1-5

Contents

Best BIG Jokes for Kids

As kids grow older they find certain jokes less and less funny. This means you have to come up with age appropriate jokes to keep them entertained. Jokes are more than just for laughs. They also stimulate thought and educate. That does not mean you go stiff on the kids, far from it. You want jokes that are funny, corny and have some substance. Usually the really good jokes will give even you the tickles.

Kids can be pretty critical and they are not afraid to let you know *"You're just not funny!"* Here 's a bit of help for you – 618 Jokes, Brain Teasers and Tongue Twisters for kids between ages 8 and 14.   Here goes!

30 Simple Jokes for Whetting the Appetite

1. **Q:** Knock, knock. Who's there?

A: Lettuce

Q: Lettuce who?

A: Lettuce in, it's freezing out here..

2. **Q:** What do elves learn in school?

A: The elf-abet

3. **Q:** Why was 6 afraid of 7?

A: Because: 7 8 9

4. **Q.** how do you make seven an even number?

A. Take out the *s*!

5. **Q:** Which dog can jump higher than a building?

A: Any dog!!! – Buildings can't jump!

6. **Q:** Why do bananas have to put on sunscreen before they go to the beach?

A: Because they might peel!

7. **Q.** How do you make a tissue dance?

A. You put a little boogie in it.

8. **Q:** Which flower talks the most?

A: Tulips, of course, 'cause they have *two* lips!

9. **Q:** Where do pencils go for vacation?

A: Pencil-vania

10. **Q:** What did the mushroom say to the fungus?

A: You're a fun guy [fungi].

11. **Q:** Why did the girl smear peanut butter on the road?

A: To go with the traffic jam!

11. Q: What do you call cheese that's not yours?

A: Nacho cheese!

12. Q: Why are ghosts bad liars?

A: Because you can see right through them.

13. **Q:** Why did the boy bring a ladder to school?

A: He wanted to go to high school.

14. **Q:** How do you catch a unique animal?

A: You neak up on it.

Q: How do you catch a tame one?

A: Tame way.

15. **Q:** Why is the math book always mad?

A: Because it has so many problems.

16. **Q.** What animal would you not want to pay cards with?

A. Cheetah

17. **Q:** What was the broom late for school?

A: Because it over swept.

18. **Q:** What music do balloons hate?

A: Pop music.

19. **Q:** Why did the baseball player take his bat to the library?

A: Because his teacher told him to hit the books.

20. **Q:** What did the judge say when the skunk walked in the court room?
A: Odor in the court!

21. **Q:** Why are fish so smart?
A: Because they live in schools.

22. **Q:** What happened when the lion ate the comedian?
A: He felt funny!

23. **Q:** What animal has more lives than a cat?

A: Frogs, they croak every night!

24. **Q:** What do you get when you cross a snake and a pie?

A: A pie-thon!

25. **Q:** Why is a fish easy to weigh?

A: Because it has its own scales!

26. **Q:** Why aren't elephants allowed on beaches?

A: They can't keep their trunks up!

27. **Q:** How did the barber win the race?

A: He knew a shortcut!

28. **Q:** Why was the man running around his bed?

A: He wanted to catch up on his sleep.

29. **Q:** Why is 6 afraid of 7?

A: Because 7 8 9!

.

30. **Q:** What is a butterfly's favorite subject at school?
A: Mothematics.

Jokes by Categories

20 Mixed Animal Jokes

Have you heard the one about a cat

Animal jokes are some of the funniest jokes around. Here are a few jokes about different animals. Specific groups will have a fun fact that be shared before going into the jokes.

1. **Q:** What do you call a sleeping bull?

A: A bull-dozer.

2. **Q:** What to polar bears eat for lunch?

A: Ice berg-ers!

3. **Q:** What do you get from a pampered cow?

A: Spoiled milk.

4. **Q:** What do you call a bear with no teeth?

A: A gummy bear!

5. **Q:** Why are teddy bears never hungry?

A: They are always stuffed!

6. **Q:** What bird is always sad?

A: The blue jay!

7. **Q.** What did the porcupine say to the cactus?

A. "Is that you mommy?

8. **Q.** Why do sea-gulls fly over the sea?

A. Because if they flew over the bay they would be bagels!

9. **Q:** Why did the snake cross the road?

A: To get to the other ssssssside!

10. Knock Knock!

Who's there?

Kook!

Kook who?

Don't call me cuckoo!

11. **Q.** What did the fish say when he swam into the wall?

A. Dam!

12. **Q:** Why are frogs so happy?

A: Because they eat what bugs them!

13. **Q:** What do you get when you cross a walrus with a bee?

A: A wallaby!

14. **Q:** What's the most musical part of a chicken?

A: The drumstick!

15. **Q:** Why didn't the dinosaur cross the road?

A: There were no roads back then!

16. **Q:** A rooster laid an egg on a barn roof. Which way would it roll?

A: Roosters don't lay eggs, hens do!

17. **Q:** Why don't oysters share their pearls?

A: Because they're shellfish!

18. **Q:** What do you call a girl with a frog in her hair?

A: Lily!

19. **Q:** What types of horses only go out at night?

A: Nightmares!

20. **Q:** Someone said you sounded like an owl.

A: Who?

10 Chicken Jokes

Fun fact: The sounds they make are actually their language (chicken language). Each alarm cry is different, and made to signify the type of predator that is threatening them.

1. **Q:** How do chickens bake a cake?

A: From scratch!

2. **Q:** Where do tough chickens come from?

A: Hard-boiled eggs!

3. **Q:** What do you get if you cross a cocker spaniel, a poodle and a rooster?

A: Cockerpoodledoo!

4. **Q:** What do you get if you cross a chicken with a cow?

A: Roost beef!

5. **Q:** Chickens rise when the rooster crows, but when do ducks get up?

A: At the quack of dawn!

6. **Q:** Why do hens lay eggs?

A: If they dropped them, they'd break!

7. **Q:** What does an evil hen lay?

A: Deviled eggs!

8. **Q:** Why did the hen cross the road?

A: To prove she wasn't a chicken!

9. **Q.** What day do chickens hate most?

A. Fry-days!

10. **Q.** Which side of a chicken has more feathers?

A. The outside.

10 Fish Jokes

Fun fact: As it relates to their to their body size, fish have small brains compared to that of most other animals.

1. **Q:** Where do fish sleep?

A: On a seabed!

2. **Q:** What do you get when you cross a shark and a snowman?

A: Frostbite!

3. **Q:** What's the most musical part of a fish?

A: The scales!

4. **Q:** What's the difference between a piano and a fish?

A: You can tune a piano, but you can't tuna fish.

5. **Q:** How do oysters call their friends?

A: On shell phones!

6. **Q:** What is the strongest creature in the sea?

A: A mussel!

.

7. **Q:** Where do fish keep their money?

A: In a river-bank!

8. **Q:** What do fish and maps have in common?

A: They both have scales!

9. **Q:** What lives in the ocean, is grouchy and hates neighbors?

A: A hermit crab!

10. **Q:** What do you call a fish without an eye?
A: fsh!

10 Cat Jokes

Fun fact: A cat whips its tail when it's in a bad mood. That means it's best for you to keep your distance!

1. **Q:** What kind of cats like to go bowling?

A: Alley cats!

2. **Q:** What is a cat's favorite color?

A: Purr-ple!

3. **Q:** What game did the cat like to play with the mouse?

A: Catch!

4. **Q:** Who was the first cat to fly in an airplane?

A: Kitty-hawk

5. **Q:** Why are cats good at video games?

A: Because they have nine lives!

.6. **Q:** What animal is bad to play games with?

A: A cheetah!

7. **Q:** What did the cat have for breakfast?

A: Mice Crispies!

8. **Q:** Why can't a leopard hide?

A: Because it's always spotted!

9. **Q:** What state has a lot of cats and dogs?

A: Petsylvania

10. **Q:** Have you ever seen a catfish?

A: No. I don't think he could he hold the rod and reel?

10 Dog Jokes

Fun fact: The shape of a dog's face gives a hint about how long it will live. Those with sharp, pointed faces (wolf-like) usually live longer than those with flat faces.

1. **Q:** What do you call a dog that is left handed?

A: A south paw!

2. **Q:** Why did the snowman call his dog "Frost"?

A: Because Frost-bites!

3. **Q:** When is a dog not a dog?

A: When it is pure bred/bread!

4. **Q:** Why did the poor dog chase its own tail?

A: It was trying to make ends meet.

5. **Q:** What do you get when you cross a sheep dog with a rose?

A: A collie-flower.

6. **Q:** Why didn't the dog speak to its foot?

A: Because it is not polite to speak back to your paw.

7. **Q:** What did the dog say when he sat on the sandpaper?

A: Ruff!

8. **Q:** What did one flee say to the other?

A: Should we walk or take a dog?

9. **Q:** What's worse than raining cats and dogs?

A: Hailing Taxis!

10. **Q:** How do you call a dog with no legs?

A: It doesn't matter how you call him. He still won't come!

10 Bear Jokes

Fun Fact: Some Native Americans call bears "the beast that walks like a man," because they can walk short distances on their hind legs.

1. **Q:** What is a bear's favorite drink?

A: Koka-Koala!

2. **Q:** What do you call bears with no ears?

A: B!

3. **Q:** Why do bears have fur coats?

A: Because they look silly wearing jackets!.

4. **Q:** How do you start a teddy bear race?

A: Teddy, Set, Go!

5. **Q:** How do Teddy bears send their letters?

A: By bear mail!

6. **Q:** What color socks do bears wear?

A: They don't wear socks, they have bear feet!

7. **Q:** What do teddy bears do when it rains?

A: They get wet!

8. **Q:** What do you get if you cross a grizzly bear with a harp?

A: A bear faced lyre!

9. **Q:** How do teddies keep their houses cool in the summer?

A: They use bear conditioning!

10. **Q:** What do bears buy when they go to the shops?

A: They buy the bear necessities!

10 Elephant Jokes

Fun fact: Of all the mammals in the world only one cannot jump, and that is the elephant.

1. Q. Why doesn't the elephant use a computer?

A. Because it is afraid of the mouse!

2. **Q:** What game do you NOT want to play with an elephant?

A: Squash!

3. **Q:** How do you stop an elephant from charging?

A: Take away her credit card!

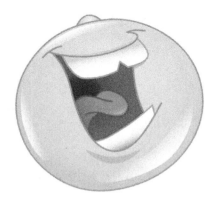

Peter MacDonald

4. **Q.** Why do elephants need trunks?

A. Because they don't have glove compartments!

.

5. Q. What's big and grey with red spots?

A. An elephant with the measles!

.

6. **Q:** Why are elephants so wrinkled?

A: They take too long to iron!

7. **Q:** How do elephants talk to each other long distance?

A: On the elephone! They make trunk calls.

8. **Q:** Why are elephants so poor?

A: Because they work for peanuts!

9. **Q:** What do elephants do in the evenings?

A: Watch elevision!

10. **Q:** What does a doctor give an elephant who's going to be sick?

A: Plenty of room!.

10 *Cow Jokes*

Fun fact: A female cattle that has given birth is called a cow while one that has not given birth is called a heifer.

1. **Q:** What do you call a cow with no legs ?

A: Ground Beef!

2. **Q:** Why does a milking stool have only three legs?

A: Because it the cow has the udder!

3. **Q:** Why do cows wear bells?

A: Their horns don't work.

4. **Q:** What do cows get when they get sick?

A: Hay fever!

5. **Q:** Where do cows go on a Friday night?

A: To the moo-vies!

6. **Q:** What happened to the lost cattle?

A: Nobody's herd!

7. **Q:** What do you get when you cross a cow and a goat?

A: A coat!

8. **Q:** What did the cow look wearing a horse costume?

A: Udderly ridiculous!!!

9. **Q:** What did the farmer call the cow that had no milk?

A: An udder failure!

10. Knock Knock!

Who's there?

Cowsgo

Cowsgo who? No they don't, cows-go moo.

10 Math Jokes

1. **Q:** Why didn't the quarter roll down the hill with the nickel?

A: Because it had more cents.

2. **Q:** What do you get when you divide the circumference of a Jack-o-lantern by its diameter?

A: Pumpkin Pi!

3. **Q:** What snakes are good at doing sums?

A: Adders!

4. **Q:** Teacher: Why are you doing your multiplication on the floor?

A: Student: You told me not to use tables.

5. **Q:** What is a math teacher's favorite sum?

A: Summer!

6. **Q:** What kind of meals do math teachers eat?

A: Square meals!

7. **Q:** What did zero say to the number eight?

A: Nice belt.

8. **Q:** Why did the two 4's skip lunch?

A: They already 8!

9. **Q:** What is a mathematician's favorite dessert?

A: Pi!

10. **Q:** If you had 8 apples in one hand and 5 apples in the other, what would you have?

A: Really big hands!

15 Food Jokes

1. **Q:** Why was the cucumber mad?

A: Because it was in a pickle!

2. **Q:** What do you call cheese that's not yours?

A: Nacho cheese!

3. **Q:** What's wrong with a restaurant on the moon?

A: It has no atmosphere!

4. **Q:** What did the nut say when it sneezed?

A: Cashew!

5. **Q:** What does a mixed up hen lay?

A: Scrambled eggs!

6. **Q:** What bird is with you every time you eat?

A: A swallow!

7. **Q:** Why did the banana have to leave in a hurry?

A: Because it had to split!

8. **Q:** What do you get when you cross a frog and a popsicle?

A: A hopsicle!

9. **Q:** What kind of plates do they use in space?

A: Flying saucers!

10. **Q:** What do ghosts like for dessert?

A: I scream!

11. **Q:** What day do potatoes hate the most?

A: Fry-day!

12. **Q:** What do sea monsters eat for lunch?

A: Fish and ships!

13. **Q:** Why was the cookie sad?

A: Because her mom was a-wafer so long!

14. **Q:** What do snowmen like to eat for breakfast?

A: Frosted Flakes!

15. **Q:** Why was the strawberry sad?

A: Because her mom was in a jam!

15 Doctor and Dentists Jokes

1. **Q:** Why did the house go to the doctor?

A: Because it had a window pain!

2. **Q:** How does a frog feel when she has a broken leg?

A: Unhoppy!

3. **Q:** Where do ghosts go when they're sick?

A: To the witch doctor!

4. **Q:** Why did the pillow go to the doctor?

A: He was feeling all stuffed up!

5. **Q:** Why didn't the girl tell the doctor that she ate some glue?

A: Her lips were sealed!

6. **Q:** What did on tonsil say to the other tonsil?

.A: Get dressed up, the doctor is taking us out

7. **Q:** When does a doctor get mad?

A: When he runs out of patients!

8. **Q:** What do you give a sick bird?

A: Tweet-ment!

9. **Q:** Did you hear the one about the germ?

A: Never mind, I don't want to spread it around

10. **Patient:** I feel like everyone is ignoring me.

Doctor: Next!

11. **Patient:** Doctor, I think I need glasses!

Waiter: You certainly do, this is a restaurant!

12. **Patient:** Doctor, sometimes I feel like I'm invisible.

Doctor: Who said that?

13. **Patient:** I think I'm a pair of curtains!

Doctor: Pull yourself together!

14. **Patient:** Doctor, I keep hearing a ringing sound.

Doctor: Then answer the phone!

15. **Patient:** I swallowed a lot of food coloring.

Doctor: You'll be okay.

Patient: But I feel like I've dyed a little inside!

20 Monster Jokes

1. **Q:** Why are graveyards noisy?

A: Because of all the coffin!

2. **Q:** What position does a ghost play in soccer?

A: Ghoulie!

3. **Q:** What do witches put on their bagels?

A: Scream cheese!

4. **Q:** Where does Dracula keep his money?

A: In a blood bank!

5. **Q:** What monster plays tricks on Halloween?

A: Prank-enstein!

6. **Q:** How does a witch tell time?

A: With a witch watch!

7. **Q:** What did the skeleton order for dinner?

A: Spare ribs!

8. **Q:** Who won the skeleton beauty contest?

A: No body!

9. **Q:** Where do baby ghosts go during the day?

A: Dayscare!

10. **Q:** What do witches put on their hair?

A: Scare spray!

11. **Q:** What breed of dog does Dracula have?

A: A bloodhound!

12. **Q:** What's a monster's favorite play?

A: Romeo and Ghouliet!

13. **Q:** Why did the vampire get thrown out of the haunted house?

A: Because he was a pain in the neck!

14. **Q:** Which circus performers can see in the dark?

A: The acro-bats!

15. **Q:** What do ghosts use to clean their hair?

A: Sham-boo!

16. **Q:** What's a ghosts favorite desert?

A: BOO- berry pie!

17. **Q:** Where do ghosts collect their letters?

A: At the GHOST office

18. **Q:** What do baby ghosts wear on their feet?

A: BOO-tees

19. **Q:** Where do ghosts buy their food?

A: At the ghost-ery store.

20. **Q:** What did the boy ghost say to the girl ghost?

A: You look boo-tiful tonight.

10 Color Jokes

1. **Q :** What's orange and sounds like a parrot?

A: A carrot!

2. **Q:** What is a cheerleader's favorite color?

A: Yeller!

3. **Q:** What color is a ghost?

A: Boo!

4. **Q:** What's blue and smells like red paint?

A: Blue paint.

.

5. **Q:** What color is an echo?

A: YELL-ooohhhhhhhhhhhhhhhh!

6. **Q:** What color is a marriage?

A: Wed

7. **Q:** What color is a baby ghost?

A: Baby boo Yellow!

8. **Q:** What color is a police investigation?

A: Copper!

9. **Q:** What do you do when you find a blue elephant?

A: Cheer her up!

10. **Q:** What happens when you throw a white hat into the Black Sea?

A: It gets wet!

10 Body Jokes

1. **Q:** How do you make a skeleton laugh?

A: Tickle her funny bone!

2. **Q:** What smells the best at dinner?

A: Your nose!

3. **Q:** What did the left eye say to the right eye?

A: Something between us smells!

4. **Q:** What's the most musical bone?

A: The trom-bone!

5. **Q:** What was served to the cannibal who was late to dinner?

A: They gave her the cold shoulder!

6. **Q:** What kind of hair do oceans have?

A: Wavy!

7. **Q:** What kind of flower grows on your face?

A: Tulips!

8. **Q:** Why didn't the skeleton cross the road?

A: It didn't have the guts!

9. **Q:** What has one eye but cannot see?

A: A needle!

10. **Q:** Did you pick your nose?

A: No, I was born with it!

10 Clothes Jokes

1. **Q:** What does a cloud wear under her raincoat?

A: Thunderwear!

2. **Q:** What are a ghost's favorite pants?

A: Boo jeans!

3. **Q:** What's the biggest problem with snow boots?

A: They melt!

4. **Q:** What kind of ties do pigs wear?

A: Pigs-ties!

5. **Q:** Where do frogs leave their hats and coats?

A: In the croakroom!

6. **Q:** What did the shoes say to the hat?

A: You go on a-head, I'll follow you on foot!

7. **Q:** What is the difference between a nicely-dressed man on a tricycle and a poorly dressed man on a bicycle?

A: A tire!

8. **Q:** What do penguins wear on their heads?

A: Ice caps!

9. **Q:** What goes up when the rain comes down?

A: An umbrella!

10. **Q:** What did the baseball glove say to the baseball?

A: Catch you later!

30 More Random Jokes

1. **Q:** What did the judge say when the skunk walked in the court room?

A: Odor in the court!

2. **Q:** Where do sheep get their wool cut?

A: At the BAAAbars!

3. **Q:** What happened to the cat that swallowed a ball of wool?

A: She had mittens!

4. **Q:** Why is the crab in prison?

A: Because he kept pinching things!

5. **Q:** Why shouldn't you tell a secret on a farm?

A: Because the potatoes have eyes and the corns have ears!

6. **Q:** What has four legs but cannot walk?

A: A chair!

7. **Q:** Why is a horse like a wedding?

A: Because they both need a groom!

8. **Q:** What is a witches' favorite subject in school?

A: Spelling!

9. **Q:** Why did the grasshopper go to the doctor?

A: Because he felt jumpy!

10. **Q.** What did the grape do when it got stepped on?

A. It let out a little wine!

11. **Q:** What did the polite ghost say to her son?

A: Don't spook until you're spoken to!

12. **Q:** What kind of roads do ghosts haunt?

A: Dead ends!

13. **Q:** Why were the early days of history called the dark ages?

A: Because there were so many knights!

14. **Q:** What kind of lighting did Noah use for the ark?

A: Floodlights!

15. **Q:** Who built the ark?

A: I have Noah idea!

16. **Q:** What did the hurricane say to the other hurricane?

A: I have my eye on you!

17. **Q:** Why couldn't the snake talk?

A: He had a frog in his throat!

.

18. **Q:** What key won't open any door?

A: A monkey!

19. **Q:** Where do chimps get their gossip?

A: On the ape vine!

20. **Q:** Why are frogs so happy?

A: Because they eat what bugs them!

21. **Q:** What did one wall say to the other wall?

A: I'll meet you at the corner.

22. **Q:** A man arrived on Friday in a small town. He stayed for two days and left on Friday. How is this possible?

A: His horse's name is Friday!

23. **Q:** What did the paper say to the pencil?

A: Write on!

24. **Q:** What goes up and down but does not move?

A: Stairs

25. **Q:** Why couldn't the pirate play cards?

A: Because he was sitting on the deck!

26. **Q:** Why can't your nose be 12 inches long?

A: Because then it would be a foot!

27. **Q:** Why was the belt arrested?

A: Because it held up some pants!

28. **Q:** Why do you go to bed every night?

A: Because the bed won't come to you!

29. **Q:** What gets wetter the more it dries?

A: A towel.

30. **Q:** Why did the robber take a bath before robbing the bank?

A: He wanted to make a clean get away!

.

About Knock Knock Jokes

Knock Jokes have been around for years, They say the first known knock knock jokes were recorded in 1936.

Knock Knock Jokes are a clever play on words, or sounds that words make. They appeal to us because of the obscure abd sometimes cryptic meanings.

Best of all they are just plain funny.

I hope you have a load of laughs as you read this section

Knock Knock!

Who's there?

Canoe!

Canoe who?

Canoe come over and play.

Knock Knock!

Who's there?

Abby!

Abby who?

Abby birthday to you.

Knock Knock!

Who's there?

Interrupting cow.

Interrupt...

Moo! (Say moo before the asker can complete the question "Interrupt cow who?")

Knock knock!

Who's there?

Little old lady?

Little old lady who?

Wow! I didn't know you could yodel!

Knock Knock!

Who's there?

Boo!

Boo who?

Don't cry, Easter Bunny comes back next year!

Knock, knock.

Who's there?
Scold.
Scold who?
S'cold out here!

Knock, knock.

69

Who's there?
The dog.
The dog who

The dog doesn't go who, the dog goes woof!.

Knock, knock.
Who's there?
Boo.
Boo who?
Oh, don't get sad and cry, it's just a joke!

Knock, knock.
Who's there?
Interrupting sheep.
Interrupting she...
Baaaaaaaaaa!

Knock, knock.
Who's there?
Who.

Who Who?

Why are you acting like an owl if you are not one?

Knock, knock.

Who's there?

Where what.

Where what who?

You sound a bit confused.

Knock, knock.

Who's there?

Figs.

Figs who?

Figs the bell and I will no longer have to knock.

Knock, knock.

Who's there?

Abbott.

Abbott who?

Abbott the right time to answer your door.

Knock, knock.

Who's there?

Ada.

Ada who?

Ada burger for dinner.

Knock, knock.

Who's there?

Broccoli.

Broccoli who?

Since when does broccoli have a last name?

Knock, knock.

Who's there?

Olive.

Olive who?

Olive right across the street.

Knock, knock.
Who's there?
Interrupting pirate.
Interrupting pir…
Arrrrrrrghhh!

Knock, knock.
Who's there?
Agatha.
Agatha who?
Agatha very bad headache. Do you have some pills?

Knock, knock.
Who's there?
Aida.
Aida who?
Aida lot of pizza and now my tummy hurts.

Knock, knock.
Who's there?
Al.
Al who?
Al give you a hug, just open that door, please!

Knock, knock.
Who's there?
Phillip.
Phillip who?
Phillip my bag with candy and chocolate!

Knock, knock.
Who's there?
Who who who.
Who who who who?
Why are you being so rude?

Knock, knock.

Who's there?

Lettuce.

Lettuce who?

Lettuce in, it's freezing out here!

Knock, knock.

Who's there?

Toaf.

Toaf who?

Tofu? What's wrong with eating meat?.

.

Knock, knock.

Who's there?

Cows.

Cows who?

Oh, no, cows don't who, cows go moo!.

Knock, knock.
Who's there?
Cash.
Cash who?
Oh thank, you, but I prefer walnuts!

Knock, knock.
Who's there?
Ken.
Ken who?
Ken I come in?.

Knock, knock.
Who's there?
Aldo.
Aldo who?
Aldo anything for you!

Knock, knock.
Who's there?
Merry.
Merry who?
Merry Christmas to all of you!

Knock, knock.
Who's there?
Needle.
Needle who?
Needle little food and a little money.

Knock, knock.
Who's there?

Roach.

Roach who?

I roach you a long letter, did you get it?

Knock, knock.

Who's there?

Etch.

Etch who?

Bless you!

Knock, knock.

Who's there?

Anee.

Anee who?

Anee one you like!

Knock, knock.
Who's there?
Nana.
Nana who?
It's nana your business.

Knock, knock.
Who's there?
Claire.
Claire who?
Claire the way, I am Coooming Thru!

Knock, knock.
Who's there?
Ya
Ya who?
Sure glad that you are so excited to see me!

Knock, knock.
Who's there?
Justin.
Justin who?
Justin the city and I came to visit you.

Knock, knock.
Who's there?
Alex.
Alex who?
Alex the questions here, this is not your job!

Knock, knock.
Who's there?
Ali.
Ali who?
Alligator!

Knock, knock.
Who's there?
Allied!
Allied who?
Allied, ok? Why don't you sue me?

Knock, knock.
Who's there?
Ashee.
Ashee who?
Oh, bless you!

Knock, knock.

Who's there?

Nobel.

Nobel who?

Nobel, that's why I am knocking on your door.

Knock, knock.

Who's there?

Lettuce.

Lettuce who?

Well, lettuce in and you will soon find out!

Knock, knock.

Who's there?

Anita.

Anita who?

Anita borrow a cup of sugar from you.

Knock, knock.
Who's there?
Annie.
Annie who?
Annie thing that you can do, I can do much better than you!

Knock, knock.
Who's there?
Cher.
Cher who?
Cher would be nice if you come out here!

Knock, knock.
Who's there?
Amarillo.
Amarillo who?
Amarillo nice girl/guy.

Knock, knock.
Who's there?
Althea.
Althea who?
Althea, if you are nice to me!

Knock, knock.
Who's there?
Alva.
Alva who?
Alva pear.

Knock, knock.
Who's there?
Amana.
Amana who?
Amana a really bad mood today!

Knock, knock.
Who's there?
Mickey.
Mickey who?
Mickey doesn't fit in the lock and this is why you have to open the door.

Knock, knock.
Who's there?
Ice cream.
Ice cream who?
Ice cream if you don't open the door.

Knock, knock.
Who's there?
Luke.
Luke who?
If you luke through the keyhole, you will see!

Knock, knock.
Who's there?
Amy.
Amy who?
Amy fraid of the dark. Please let me in!

Knock, knock.
Who's there?
Andrew.
Andrew who?
Andrew a picture of you!.

Knock, knock.
Who's there?
Kent.
Kent who?
Kent you tell by the sound of my voice?.

Knock, knock.
Who's there?
Isabel.
Isabel who?
Isabel working? I had to knock on the door first.

Knock, knock.
Who's there?
Carl.
Carl who?
Car'l get you there much faster than a bike would.

Knock, knock.
Who's there?
Tiss.
Tiss who?
Oh, do you have a cold?

Knock, knock.
Who's there?
Radio.
Radio who?
Radio not, here I come!

Knock, knock.
Who's there?
Annie.
Annie who?
Annie one just like you!

Knock, knock.
Who's there?
Arthur.
Arthur who?
Arthur any more people like you?

Knock, knock.
Who's there?
Dishes.
Dishes who?
Dishes the police, open the door!

Knock, knock.
Who's there?
Arbus.
Arbus who?
Arbus leaves in 10 minutes, hurry up!

Knock, knock.
Who's there?
Evvie.
Evvie who?
Evvie thing I do, I do for you!

Knock, knock.
Who's there?
Doughnut.
Doughnut who?
Doughnut ask me questions, come out and see for yourself!

Knock, knock.
Who's there?
Atlas.
Atlas who?
Atlas its Saturday!

Knock, knock.
Who's there?
Bean.
Bean who?
Bean to the market lately?

Knock, knock.

Who's there?

Bera

Bera who?

Bera necessities!

Knock, knock.

Who's there?

Shelby.

Shelby who?

Shelby coming around the mountain when she comes!

Knock, knock.

Who's there?

Dewey.

Dewey have to keep on telling these knock knock jokes?

.

Knock, knock.
Who's there?
I-8.
I-8 who?
I-8 breakfast already. Are we going to have lunch?

Knock, knock.
Who's there?
I love.
I love who?
Why who, I love you!

Knock, knock.
Who's there?
Norma Lee.
Normal Lee who?
Norma Lee I don't knock, I ring the bell.

Knock, knock.
Who's there?
Your mama.
Your mama who?
It's really your mama, baby, open the door!

Knock, knock.
Who's there?
Howie.
Howie who?
Howie going to get inside?

Knock, knock.
Who's there?
Hawaii.
Hawaii who?
I'm fine, thank you, Hawaii you?

Knock, knock.
Who's there?
Betty.
Betty who?
Betty you can't really tell who it is!

Knock, knock.
Who's there?
Ben.
Ben who?
Ben wondering what you are about to do.

Knock, knock.
Who's there?
Pecan.
Pecan who?
Hey, pecan somebody your own size!.

Knock, knock.
Who's there?
Repeat.
Repeat who?
Who, who!

Knock, knock.
Who's there?
Eileen.
Eileen who?
Eileen on the door and I break it!

Knock, knock.
Who's there?
Cereal.
Cereal who?
Cereal, real nice pleasure to meet you!

Knock, knock.
Who's there?
Orange.
Orange who?
Orange you glad to see me?

Knock, knock.
Who's there?
Banana split.

93

Banana split who?
Banana split so ice creamed!

Knock, knock.
Who's there?
Theodore.
Theodore who?
Theodore's stuck and I can't open it!

Knock, knock.
Who's there?
Carrie.
Carrie who?
Carrie the garbage to the trash bean, please!

Knock, knock.
Who's there?
Cash.
Cash who?
Cash me if you can.

Knock, knock.
Who's there?
Tank.
Tank who?
You are more than welcome!

Knock, knock.
Who's there?
Harry.
Harry who?
Harry up and open the door!

Knock, knock.
Who's there?
Butter.
Butter who?
I butter not tell you or you'll get mad!

Knock, knock.
Who's there?
I scream.
I scream who?
I scream with chocolate sauce!

Knock, knock.
Who's there?
Lass
Lass who?
Oh, are you a cowboy?

Knock, knock.
Who's there?
Callum.
Callum who?
I'll Callum back.

Knock, knock.

Who's there?

Never.

Never who?

Never mind.

Knock, knock.

Who's there?

Icon.

Icon who?

Icon tell you but why don't you guess?.

Knock, knock.

Who's there?

Despair.

Despair who?

Despair tire just went flat and I can't drive home.

Knock, knock.
Who's there?
Ice cream.
Ice cream who?
Ice cream every time I see you.

Knock, knock.
Who's there?
Chile.
Chile who?
Chile out!

Knock, knock.
Who's there?
A little girl (boy).
A little girl (boy) who?
A little girl (boy) who can't reach the doorbell!

Knock, knock.
Who's there?
Chopin.
Chopin who?
Chopin in the supermarket.

Knock, knock.
Who's there?
Abbey.
Abbey who?
Abbey stung me on the arm!

Knock, knock.
Who's there?
Carlotta.
Carlotta
Carlotta trouble every time it breaks down!

Knock, knock.
Who's there?
Jilly.
Jilly who?
It's really Jilly out here, let me in!

Knock, knock.
Who's there?
Ben.
Ben who?
Ben away for a long, long time!

Peter MacDonald

Knock, knock.
Who's there?
Dozen.
Dozen who?
Dozen anyone want to let me in?

Knock, knock.
Who's there?
Adore.
Adore who?
Adore is between the two of us.

Knock, knock.
Who's there?
Two-knee.
Two-knee who?
A can of two-knee fish!

Knock, knock.
Who's there?
Honey bee.
Honey bee who?
Honey bee a dear and open the door for me!

Knock, knock.
Who's there?
A heard.
A heard who?
A heard you were in town so I decided to come by!

Knock, knock.
Who's there?
Iva.
Iva who?
Iva runny nose from the cold out here, open the door!

Knock, knock.
Who's there?
Canoe.
Canoe who?
Canoe help me with the shopping?

Knock, knock.

Who's there?

Noah.

Noah who?

Noah good pizza place. Want to go for lunch?

Knock, knock.

Who's there?

Owls.

Owls who?

But of course owls who, what else would they do?

Knock, knock.

Who's there?

Chuck.

Chuck who?

Chuck the door, is it locked?

Knock, knock.
Who's there?
Water.
Water who?
Water you doing there, this is my house?

Knock, knock.
Who's there?
Sasha.
Sasha who?
Sasha fuzz! I just knocked on the door!

Knock, knock.
Who's there?
Ears.
Ears who?
Ears a lot more of those knock knock jokes for you!

Knock, knock.
Who's there?
Ralph.
Ralph who?
Ralph, Ralph, Ralph! I'm the dog!

Knock, knock.
Who's there?
B-4.
B-4 who?
Open the door B-4 I freeze!

Knock, knock.
Who's there?
Spell.
Spell who?
Oh, that's easy – W, H, and O!

Knock, knock.
Who's there?
Tennis who?
Tennis easy – five plus five!

Knock, knock.
Who's there?
Costa.
Costa who?
Costa lot to repair the doorbell!

Will you remember me in an hour?
Yes!
Will you remember me in a day?
Yes!
Will you remember me in a month?
Yes!
Knock, knock.
Who's there?
See, you already forgot me!

Best Brain Teasers

For Kids

Good
Clean
Fun

68 Best Brain Teasers For Kids

Brain teasers are word puzzles that may be spoken or written and they require you to use mental reasoning to find the answer to the puzzle. Generally, you only need your brain to solve these puzzles.

Basically, using brain teasers is like doing a workout specifically for your brain. The more you work your brain, the stronger and more developed it becomes.

Benefits of Brain Teasers

Brain teasers offer a number of benefits, especially for children. Studies show that playing mind games, such as brain teasers, can increase blood flow to the brain, increasing the performance of the brain.

The increase in blood flow also results in important chemical changes that result in improved brain function.

Using brain teasers regularly offers a fun way that children can improve cognitive skills, such as comprehension, memory, attention, perception, language skills and more. Brain teasers help to improve alertness and concentration in children. They help to activate the thinking process, exercising and stimulating the mind.

Since brain teasers are fun and exciting, children can have a great time while exercising their brain and developing improved mental skills.

Brain teasers are fun to do alone, or they can be done as a team to encouraging working together.

Some children even enjoy competing against friends to see who is able to figure out the right answer first.

Easy Brain Teasers

Starting out with easy brain teasers is a great way to begin getting your brain in shape. Easy brain teasers help warm up the brain, training your brain and making it stronger.

Start working on these simple brain teasers before you move on to harder ones. Once you find it easy to solve the easy brain teasers, then you can go on to moderately hard teasers, working your way up to difficult ones.

The following are some easy brain teasers to get you started.

1 – An electric train is traveling north. The wind is blowing from the south-west. Which way is the smoke from the train blowing?

2 – Sam, Kevin, Nick, Henry and Brian were all taking a walk around a big lake while they were on vacation during the rainy season.

Brian was wearing a waterproof cap and a raincoat.

Henry and Kevin both were comfortable with the umbrellas they were carrying. Henry gave his umbrella to Sam.

However, no one gave poor Nick anything to protect himself from the rain. However, Nick did not get wet. How is this possible?

3 – How is it possible to make libraries bigger without building anything?

4 – What animals have the best education?

5 – What is unable to run, even though it has three feet?

6 – How can you make an egg roll?

7 – If five dollars are on the table and I take three dollars away, how many dollars will I have?

8 – Penguins can move as fast as five miles per hour. How long will it take a penguin to fly 80 miles?

9 – A father and son were driving and they ended up in a car accident.

They were taken to two separate hospitals.

The son was ready for an operation when the surgeon suddenly said, "I cannot operate on him. He is my son!"

Who was the surgeon?

10 – A barrel is filled with water and it weighs 120 pounds. A man puts something into the barrel and now weighs less than 120 pounds. What did the man put in the barrel?

11 – Jimmy has two U.S coins. The two coins total fifty-five cents. One is not a nickel. What coins does Jimmy have?

12 – Farmer Dan had 10 sheep. All but eight died.

How many sheep does farmer Dan have left?

13 – Some months have as many as 31 days while others have 30 days.

How many months have 28 days?

14 – What word is always spelled wrong?

15 – Eight children were walking to the bookstore.

All but two decided to stop at the ice cream parlor instead.

How many children made it to the bookstore?

16 – Two men are playing checkers.

They each play seven complete games.

Both men win the same number of checkers games. No ties occur.

How is this possible?

17 – You are running a marathon.

As you are running, you finally overtake the person who is in 2nd place.

What place are you currently in?

18 – A rooster is laying eggs on the rooftop.

Which way do those eggs roll?

19 – A fire broke out in a 15 story building.

A woman gets scared and panics, jumping out of the window to escape the fire.

She survives. How?

20 – You can catch it but you cannot throw it. What is it?

Peter MacDonald

21 – When you take my skin off, I do not cry. However, you may cry. What am I?

22 – Which word does not belong in this group?

First, Second, Third, Forth, Fifth, Sixth, Seventh, Eighth, Ninth

23 – My top and bottom both have holes.
I have holes in the middle and on the sides too. However, I can still hold water.

Can you guess what I am?

Moderately Hard Brain Teasers

Once you have mastered easy brain teasers, it's time to start challenging your brain a bit more.

Enjoy a tougher challenge by trying out these moderately hard brain teasers.

1 – You have one match. You walk into a room and you have a wood burning stove, an oil burner and an oil lamp.

What do you light first?

2 – Henry grows cherries and decides to sell them at a local farmer's market.

3 –On a winter day, a pure white dog crosses the street.

It has been storming for hours and no one has plowed the road. People can easily see the dog. How?

He plans to charge $2.50 for each basket of cherries.

The first day he sells 15 baskets of cherries.
The second day he only sells 12. The third day he has a great day and sells 35. The fourth day is rainy and he only sells 3. The fifth day he sells 10. The sixth day he sells 18. Then, on the seventh day, he sells 22 and three quarters.

How many baskets of strawberries does he sell in seven days?

4 – A cyclist crosses the French and Spanish border every single day.

He always carries a bag. However, no matter how many times he is searched and investigated, they cannot figure out what he's smuggling.

Can you figure out what he is smuggling?

5 – A man is captive in an island prison.

He does not know how to swim.

Finally, he escapes from the prison and has nothing but himself.

There is not a bridge to help him.

How did the man escape from the prison?

6 – A woman was speeding and she ran right through a stop sign.

There were two police officers that saw it happen but they simply sat there and did nothing.

Why?

7 – Pinkie Pinkerton was living in a beautiful, pink, one story

home that was located on Pink Street.

The roof, the carpet, the pictures, the furniture, the walls, the bathroom, the yard and the flowers were all pink.

Everything in the house was pink.

What color was the stairway in her house?

8 – Jane walked all day long. At the end of the day, she had only move two feet.

How can this be?

9 – What can move backwards and forwards, yet it has no legs.

10 – You go into a bathroom that has no windows and stone walls.

You start to run a bath but the handles break off and you have no way to turn off the tap.

Since the door is locked on the outside and no windows are in the bathroom, you cannot escape.

The room will soon flood and you will end up drowning.

Is there a way that you can save yourself?

11 – A baseball game ends and the score is 6 to 3.

No walks occurred and no one stole any bases. No men score runs.

How could this be?

12 – Five boys were in a foot race.

Mark finished before Sam, but behind Ed. Ron finished before John, but behind Sam.

In what order did all the boys end up finishing the foot race?

13 – Jenny loves cats and has several as pets.

All but two cats are totally black. All but two are totally white. All but two happen to be completely ginger.

How many cats does Jenny have?

14 – The school orchestra has 21 musicians and they can complete Beethoven's Moonlight Sonata in just 5 minutes and 31 seconds.

If the school orchestra doubled the number of musicians, how long would it take for the orchestra to play the piece of music?

15 – I always run and I never walk. While I have a bed, I

never sleep.

Even though I have a mouth, I can't eat.

What am I?

16 – I will follow you all through the day.

When rain or night comes, I disappear.

What am I?

17 – An old cowboy rides into a small city on Friday.

The cowboy stays in the city two days and he leaves the city on Saturday.

How is this possible?

18 – I belong to you, but other people use it a lot more than you use it.

What am I?

19 – Three houses are located in a row. One house is blue, one house is white and one house is red.

The blue house is to the right of the middle house. The red house is to the left of the middle house.

Where is the white house?

20 – In a dictionary, you will always find one word that is

spelled incorrectly.

What word is it?

21 – All day long I run around over fields, streets, woods and more.

When I sit under the bed at night, I am never alone.

My tongue hangs out as I wait to be filled again in the morning.

What am I?

22 – Jane's mother has four kids.

The first child is named April, the second child is named May and the third child is named June.

What did the mother name her fourth child?

23 – You are driving a big city bus.

Five people get on and two people get off the bus.

Then, at the next stop, ten people get on the bus and 12 get off the bus.

Next, three people get off the bus and 5 people get on the bus.

Can you figure out the color of the bus driver's eyes?

24 – In Colorado, it snows 44 inches.

While you have two snow blowers, you do not have fuel for them.

Your next door neighbor living in San Francisco does have some fuel, but you do not like to talk to him.

What can you do?

25 – The Mississippi River lies right between Arkansas and Tennessee, dividing the two states.

If a plane ends up crashing right in the middle of the river, where will the survivors end up being buried?

Difficult Brain Teasers

1 – Put a coin into an empty bottle.

Then, place a cork into the bottle's neck.

Can you figure out a way to take the coin out of the bottle without breaking the bottle or taking the cork out of the bottle?

2 – A farmer comes to a river and has a fox, chicken and a bag of grain with him.

He has a boat to help get them across the river but it only will hold one other thing besides him.

However, as he takes the items across, he cannot leave the chicken and the fox together, since the fox will eat the chicken.

He cannot leave the chicken and the grain together because the chicken will eat the grain. How does the farmer manage to get all of the items across safely?

3 – Look at this paragraph. Can you find out what is unusual about it? It looks plain and you probably think nothing is wrong. Nothing is wrong with it, but it is unusual. Study it thoroughly and think. You may not find anything that is odd about it. Think about for a bit and you may find out what is unusual about this paragraph.

4 – As an old man started getting older, he decided that he wanted to leave his fortune to one of his sons.

He had three sons but he could not figure out which son he should give the fortune to.

To figure it out, he decided to give each son a little money, telling his sons they should buy something that will completely fill the living room.

The first son purchased straw, but the straw could not fill the room. The second son purchased some sticks, but they did not fill the entire room either.

The third son purchase two things and they filled the entire room, and so his father game the third son his fortune.

What did the third son buy and what filled the room?

5 – A ship is anchored within a port and it has a ladder that is hanging over the side.

The very bottom rung is touching the water.

There are six inches between each rung. The ladder is 60 inches in length.

The tide continues to rise at about five inches per hour.

At what point will the water rise enough to reach the fifth rung from the top?

6 – A young lady has been browsing for a long time. Finally, she walks up to the man behind the counter and hands the man a book.

The man looks at the inside tag and says, "That will be $3.50 please." The woman hands the man the money and then walks away, leaving the book behind.

Even though the man sees her leave without the book, he does not try to stop her. Why not?

7 – I have two arms, but fingers none. I have two feet, but cannot run. I carry well, but I have found I carry best with my feet off the ground. What am I?

8 – Pauls height is 6 feet, he's an assistant at a butchers shop, and he wears size 9 shoes.

What does he weigh?

9 – The person who makes it has no need for it.

The person who purchases it does not use it.

The person who does use it does not know he or she is.

What is it?

10 – Complete this sequence of letters:
o, t, t, f, f, s, s, _, _, _.

11 – If your sock drawer has 6 black socks, 4 brown socks, 8 white socks, and 2 tan socks, how many socks would you have to pull out in the dark to be sure you had a matching pair?

12 – Torn Suit A man was just doing his job when his suit was torn. Three minutes late he died. Why

13 –

8809 = 6

7111 = 0

2172 = 0

6666 = 4

1111 = 0

3213 = 0

7662 = 2

9312 = 1

0000 = 4

2222 = 0

3333 = 0
5555 = 0

8193 = 3

8096 = 5

7777 = 0

9999 = 4

7756 = 1

6855 = 3

9881 = 5

5531 = 0

2581 = ?

14 –A fast food restaurant sells chicken in orders of 6, 9, and 20.

What is the largest number of pieces of chicken you cannot

order from this restaurant?

15 – A woman shoots her husband.

Then she holds him under water for over 5 minutes.

Finally, she hangs him.

But 5 minutes later they both go out together and enjoy a wonderful dinner together.

How can this be?

16 – A man walks into a pub and simply orders a water.

The bar tender simply looks at the man, grabs a shotgun, and points it at the man's face.

The man says, "Thank you" gets up, and walks out of the pub.

Why did they behave this way?

17 – Why can't Kevin Smith, who is now living in Canada, not be buried in the USA?

18– Which creature walks on four legs in the morning, two legs in the afternoon, and three legs in the evening?

19 –Who spends the day at the window, goes to the table for meals and hides at night?

20 – A man is pushing his car along the road when he comes to a hotel. He shouts, "I'm bankrupt!"

Why?

Brain Teaser Answer Key:

Easy Brain Teaser Answers:

1 – There is no smoke because it is an electric train.

2 – It was not raining when Sam, Kevin, Nick, Henry and Brian were walking around the lake.

3 – Add more stories to the library.

4 – Fish. Fish travel in schools.

5 – A yard stick.

6 – Push the egg.

7 – Three dollars, because two dollars are left on the table.

8 – Penguins are not able to fly.

9 – The surgeon was the boy's mother.

10 – The man put a hole in the barrel, letting the water drain

out so the barrel weighed less.

11 – Jimmy has a half dollar and a nickel. Remember, it says that only ONE wasn't a nickel.

12 – Farmer Dan has eight sheep left.

13 – All months have 28 days.

14 – The word "wrong."

15 – Two children made it to the library.

16 – The men are not playing checkers against each other.

17 – You are in second place.

18 – Roosters cannot lay eggs.

19 – She jumps out of a window on the first floor of the building.

20 – It is a cold.

21 – I am an onion.

22 – Forth. It is spelled incorrectly for this group and should actually be spelled "fourth."

23 – I am a sponge.

Moderately Hard Brain Teaser
Answers:

1 – You light the match first before you can light anything else.

Peter MacDonald

2 – None. Henry was selling cherries, not strawberries.

3 – It's raining not snowing.

4 – He is smuggling bicycles across the border.

5 – The many escaped prison during the winter. The ice froze and he was able to walk away on the ice.

6 – The woman was running, not driving a car.

7 – There was no stairway – it is a one story house.

8 – Jane only has two feet, so she only moved two feet while walking.

9 – It is a door.

10 – All you have to do is pull the plug on the bathtub so the water will drain out.

11 – The baseball game was played by all women.

12 – Ed finished first. Mark finished second. Sam finished third. Ron finished fourth. John finished fifth.

13 – Jenny has three cats. One is black, one is white and one is ginger.

14 – The same amount of time. The length of the music piece does not change just because you add more musicians.

15 – I am a river.

16 – I am your shadow.

17 – The name of the cowboy's horse is Friday.

18 – I am your name.

19 – The White House is in Washington, DC.

20 – The word is "Incorrectly."

21 – I am a shoe.

22 – Jane.

23 – What color are your eyes? Remember, YOU are the one who is driving the bus.

24 – You do nothing. Since your neighbor lives in San Francisco, obviously you live there too. You do not need to worry about how much snow is in Colorado.

25 – Nowhere. You do not bury the survivors.

Difficult Brain Teaser Answers:

1 – Yes. You can push the cork until it falls into the bottle and then shake the bottle until the coin falls out.

2 – First, the farmer has to take the chicken to the other side, leaving the grain and fox.

Then, he goes back for the fox, drops it off and takes the chicken with him.

He takes the chicken back, picks the grain up and leaves the chicken behind.

He drops the grain off and leaves it with the fox.

He heads back and gets the chicken, heading to the other

side.

They now are all on the same side of the river.

3 – The most common letter in the alphabet, the letter "E," is not used in the entire paragraph.

4 – The third son purchased a candle and a match.

He used the match to light the candle. Light filled the entire room.

5 – If the tide starts rising, the ship continues to rise on the water.

This means that the water will still only be touching the first rung and will never actually touch the fifth rung from the top.

6 – It is a library and the young lady simply paid a fine for a book that was overdue.

7 – A wheel Barrow

8 – He weighs Meat

9 – A coffin.

10 – e, n, t - The first letter of the numbers from one to ten.

11 – Five. There are only four colors, so five socks guarantee t`hat two will be the same color.

12 – He was an astronaut on a space walk, doing repairs.

13 – 2581 = 2

14 – Answer: 43.

After 6 all numbers divisible by 3 can be ordered (because they can all be expressed as a sum of 6's and 9's). After 26, all numbers divisible by three when subtracted by 20 can be obtained. After 46, all numbers divisible by three when subtracted by 40 can be obtained. After 46, all numbers fit into one of these 3 categories, so all numbers can be obtained. 43 is the last number that doesn't fall into one of these categories (44 = 20 + 6 * 4, 45 = 6 * 6 + 9).

15 – She shot a photo of him, developed the print, and hung it up to dry.

16 – The Man had the hiccups and the bar man gave him a fright to cure him.

17 – He is alive

18 – Man. He crawls on all fours as a baby, then walks on two feet as an adult, and then walks with a cane as an old man.

19 – A fly.

20 – He was Playing Monopoly

Peter MacDonald

Best Brain Teasers

For Kids

WHO

AM

I

?

LETS HAVE SOME MORE FUN

115 Best Brain Teasers For Kids – WHO AM I?

Good
Clean
Fun

Easy

Who Am I Brain Teasers

Starting out with easy brain teasers is a great way to begin getting your brain in shape. Easy brain teasers help warm up the brain, training your brain and making it stronger. Start working on these simple brain teasers before you move on to harder ones. Once you find it easy to solve the easy brain teasers, then you can go on to moderately hard teasers, working your way up to difficult ones.

Easy "Who am I" Brain Teasers

1 – You can write me forward, backward, or even upside down, yet I still can be read from left to right. Who am I?

2 – I can be cracked, I can be made. I can be told, and I can be played. Who am I?

3 – I can be long or short and I am a tool. You can use me to survive, but whether I am good or evil depends upon the way that you use me. Who am I?

4 – I am my mother's child, my father's child, yet no one's son. Who am I?

5 – Take away my letters, yet my name will still be the same. The letters that you take I will never reclaim, since when they are gone, my name is still the same. Who am I?

6 – While you will find me in Paris, I am not found in France, and among my siblings, I happen to be the thinnest. Who am

I?

7 – I am older than the computer, and you use me all the time. Sometimes I am colorful and I have tons of fiber. Who am I?

8 – I have married many, yet I have never been married. Who am I?

9 – I am water's son, yet when I am returned to water, I will die. Who am I?

10 – I was not here yesterday, yet today I am here. Tomorrow I will not be around, but I may see you once each week. Who am I?

11 – I can be pesky and sneaky, yet when I seek the truth, I often end up in trouble. Who am I?

12 – If you say my name, I no longer exist. Who am I?

13 – Let me live, and my life will be short. However, kill me and I will stay around longer. Who am I?

14 – While I live in a little house that is filled with meat, there is no door where you can go in and eat. Who am I?

15 – People walk on me all night and day, but I never get to sleep. Who am I?

16 – I can run, yet I will never get tired. Who am I?

17 – While I can be turned up and turned low, the problem is that I cannot glow. Who am I?

18 – When I am empty, nothing will move me, but I can point the way when I am filled. Who am I?

19 – I am the one who knows all of your secrets. Who am I?

20 – I only think good things, even when bad things happen. Who am I?

21 – I live for the crowd, and I live for the laughter. If you do not laugh, I have failed. Who am I?

22 – I have a bow and arrow, and I have wings. I love my job, and at my job, hate is never spoken of. I only speak of love, and I will help you fall in love too. Who am I?

23 – I really love those peanuts, all the books say. I am becoming more endangered each and every day. I weigh nearly a ton, and I will eat a ton too. Who am I?

24 – I always play fair, and I always get dirty. A diamond is my playground. When I am nearly done, I'll run home. Who am I?

25 – I was framed. However, the person who framed me did not do anything wrong. Who am I?

26 – I am very beneficial, and many people talk about me. However, it is difficult to find me during a war. I am often found at the end of a war, and without me, the world will never survive. Who am I?

27 – While I have no wings, I fly. I do not have eyes, but I can see. Even with no arms, I can climb. I am stronger than anything and I'm responsible for the evolution of society. Who am I?

28 – My mother's name is red, and my father's name is blue. Who am I?

29 – I live in the canopy and rarely touch the ground. I move so slow and spend most of my time hanging upside down. Tree leaves are my favorite food. People often call me lazy. Who am I?

30 – When I left, I had no idea where I was going. When I arrived, I was not sure where I was. When I returned, I was not sure where I had been. Who am I?

31 – I dig out tiny holes and store silver and gold in them. I make crowns of gold and bridges of silver. Everyone needs my help, but many people are afraid of me. Who am I?

32 – Many people try to hide, and some try to cheat me. However, you and I will someday meet. Who am I.

Moderately Hard

Medium-hard "Who am I" Brain Teasers

33 – Throw me out the window and you will leave a grieving wife. Who am I?

34 – I can make you feel weak in the worst times, but I actually help keep you safe. While I may make you sweat, I will also make you cold. Both the weak and the brave know me well, but the brave have learned to act despite me. Who am I?

35 – If my neighbor makes mistakes, I will eliminate them. Who am I?

36 – I am hot and I change colors depending on my heat. While I keep eating, I am never full. Who am I?

37 – You walk on me all the time. I drink and drink, yet my thirst is never quenched. Who am I?

38 – You cannot see me, but you know I am there when I run my fingers through your hair. I can sing nearly any song. Who am I?

39 – I have thirty men, but only two women, yet it is the women that have the most power. They dress in black and white, and they often fight for hours at a time. Who am I?

Peter MacDonald

40 – I am the ruler of all the shovels and I have a wife. I also have a double, and I am as skinny as a thin knife. Who am I?

41 – I am easiest to see after night has fallen and I beautifully light up the sky. When I show off my colors I will help you celebrate the 4th of July.

42 – I am neither living or dead, yet I can change faces all the time. I attract many eyes. Who am I?

43 – My dinner guests always call us even when they realize their place in my meal. I do get a little bit fed up with people. Who am I?

44 – I was born in flame and conceived in earth. While some use me with shame, others use me with mirth. When I have been tamed, I rarely miss, and men everywhere fear my cold, deadly kiss. They cloak themselves in heavy shells and chains, and they try to avoid my inevitable pain. I am a gift fit for soldiers, yet I am also owned by kings, and my beauty rivals that on an angel's wings. Who am I?

45 – I can be black as the forest or pale as sunlight. Sometimes I am long, and sometimes I am short – the choice is yours. You choose the way I look. Who am I?

46 – I am watching you, and I judge people through the year. I do not need a car, because I have my own deer. Lucky for me, I only work one day out of every year. Who am I?

47 – The blackboard and chalk are my very best friends, and you often see me in the morning until the afternoon ends.

140

While I am really smart, some people think I'm mean, but opinions of me depend on how I am seen. Who am I?

48 – There are four houses, a blue house, a green house, a red house, and a white house. A blue man lives in the blue house, the green many lives in the green house, and the red man lives in the red house. I live in the White House. Who am I?

49 – I have a lot of teeth, but no mouth. My hands use me. I come in many sizes and colors, and you probably use me every day. Who am I?

50 – While I have an eye, I am not able to see. I have no limbs, but I am still faster and stronger than any man. Who am I?

51 – I only have one leg, yet I have three eyes. Who am I?

52 – You will find me in an orchestra. However, if a lightning bolt hit the orchestra, I am the one who would probably be hit. Who am I?

53 – I am a seven letter word. My 1st, 2nd and 3rd letters a spell a liquid. My 3rd, 4th, 5th, and 6th letters spell a type of pain. My 6th and 7th letters spell a place you find in a hospital. Who am I?

54 – When you look at me, I smile back at you. When you wink at me, I wink back at you. When you kiss me, I kiss you back. When you say, "I love you," I will say it back. Who am I?

55 – I am often known as a right, and some think I am a

reason, but everyone wants me, especially people who are trapped. Who am I?

56 – I am black and I can cause a lot of pain. I am common in children who love to eat candy. Unfortunately, you will have to pay a lot of money to get rid of me. Who am I?

57 – I am found in evil, yet I am in holy too. While I am not in heaven, I am found in hell. You can find me in excellence, but no in badness. I am neither friend nor foe, and you will not find me in misery or woe. While you can find me in lust, I am very noble too. Although I am not in greed, you will find me in wealth. Who am I?

58 – I can be no older than a month, yet I have existed for millions and millions of years. Some think I have a man, and others think I have cheese, yet today, I have neither. Who am I?

59 – When you take your first breath, you are introduced to me. I am a memory of things that have already passed. I remind you that nothing is permanent. While I am often heralded, you cannot touch me. I am a guardian and I will lead you through the unknown. People often say that I am short. Who am I?

60 – My father's name is blue. If you mix my name with my father's name, you will have maroon. If you mix me with my mom's name, I would only get a little lighter. If you mix my mother's name and my father's name, you will get my name. Who am I?

61 – You cannot see me and you cannot touch me, yet you can hear me. Who am I?

62 – Without me, you cannot live. While I am as light as a feather, you cannot hold me for very long. Who am I?

63 – I have fingers and thumbs, yet I have no bone, I have no scales, I have no feathers, and I even have no flesh. Who am I?

64 – I am the longest word that you will ever find in a dictionary. Who am I?

65 – I have no legs, but I can dance. I have no lungs, but I have to breathe to live. Who am I?

66 – I am only one color, yet I can be many sizes. I am stuck at the bottom, yet I can easily fly. You can see me when the sun is out, but the rain chases me away. I do no harm and I feel no pain. Who am I?

67 – I am a nut, yet I have no shell. Who am I?

68 – I am usually cheaper when I am young, and I can make you happy. As I grow older, I am more valued. Who am I?

69 – If you have me, you will want to share me with someone else. But, if you share me, you will not have me anymore. Who am I?

70 – The more you have of me, the less you will be able to see. Who am I?

71 – Once I was only owned by wealthy people, but soon, everyone had me. You cannot buy me in a bookstore and you cannot take me out of a library. Today, I am almost extinct. Who am I?

72 – If you take off my skin, you will not make me cry. However, when you take off my skin, I will make you cry. Who am I?

73 – The more I dry, the wetter I get. Who am I?

74 – You can never eat me for breakfast and you can never eat me for dinner. Who am I?

75 – I come from an egg, and I have no legs. I have a backbone, yet I am rarely straight. I can peel like an onion, yet I still am whole. I can be very long, and I can fit in a hole. Who am I?

76 – I am a five letter word, and I am usually under you. If you take away my first letter, I will be on top of you. If you take away my first and second letters, you will find me all around you. Who am I?

77 – I have a horn and I can give you milk, but I am not a cow. Who am I?

78 – I am tall and thin. I cannot walk, yet I have a tilted head. Who am I?

79 – At dusk I will appear without being fetched. I will

Best Mega Joke Book for Kids

disappear at dawn, but I will not be stolen. I am a guide to the sailors. Who am I?

80 – I start with the letter "E" and I also end with the letter "E." However, I usually only contain a single letter. Who am I?

81 – I am little more than holes that are tied to more holes. Even though I am not stiff like a pole, I am strong as steel.

82 – With pointed fangs, I sit and wait. With a heavy force, I dole out fate. Over my bloodless victims, I proclaim my might, eternally joining in just one bite. Who am I?

83 – When I am pointing up, everything is bright. When I am pointing down, everything is dark. Who am I?

84 – I am a fountain, yet no one can drink me. I am sought after like gold, yet my color is black. Who am I?

85 – Humans can create me, yet they cannot control me. I will suck on flesh, paper, wood and more. I am more costly than anyone ever thinks I will be. Who am I?

86 – If you take a minute to stop and look, you will always see me. You can try to touch me, but you will not be able to feel me. I cannot move, but when you move closer to me, I will always move away from you. Who am I?

87 – When you want to use me, you will throw me out. When you are done using me, you will take me in. Who am I?

88 – You can break me, but you can never touch me. Who am I?

Hard

Hard "Who am I" Brain Teasers

89 – As I age, I change stature. However, no matter how old I get, I am still important. My boss determines my importance. Once we part, I am no longer of any importance. Who am I?

90 – Some people use me to get around, but I never actually touch the ground. In some cases, I fall, yet sometimes I float. Who am I?

91 – You probably have two eyes, but I only have one. Although I have an eye, I have no eyeballs. My eye is not dangerous, yet my whole is extremely dangerous. While the air is clear where you find my eye, I cannot see. Who am I?

92 – I serve many people, depending on how healthy people are. When I am successful, most people forget about me. Who am I?

93 – Sometimes I am shaped like a banana. Sometimes I

am shaped like a sphere. Sometimes you cannot see me at all. Who am I?

94 – I am seen when the sun is high, and I am also seen in the darkest of night. You will find me in a holiday song when there is lots of snow so white. I am often used in the kitchen, and you will find me in a calendar. Who am I?

95 – I have a mouth, yet I cannot drink. I have a head, but I cannot think. I have a tongue, but I do not have a lung. Sometimes I am held, and sometimes I am hung. Who am I?

96 – I am a word and I am six letters long. Sometimes I enter with a loud gong. My letters are all in order, from A to Z, and I happen to start with the letter B. Who am I?

97 – I hear a lot and I say a lot, but most people never look for me. Very few people hear me, and I often hide in plain sight. All I want to do is help, but most people want to bend me. I often show up when I am least expected, and once I come to light, there is no place to hide from me. Who am I?

98 – I am no thicker than a finger when I fold, but I can be as thick as what I am holding when I hold. Who am I?

99 – Some people are very quick to take me, yet others must be coaxed. It is those who chose to take me who can lose or gain the most. Who am I?

100 – I am guided as I scrape along, and I leave behind a

snowy, against that which I am scraping. When I am scraping, I must. Who am I?

101 – I only can exist when I am between two things. Most people know very well all the hardship that I bring. Who am I?

102 – When I am broken, I will not make a lot of noise. People always break me on purpose. Who am I?

103 – In many ways, I am proudly shown, and many like me have been sewn. I never tear from being worn, but if I am torn, I must be burned. Who am I?

104 – I have four legs, but I cannot take a walk. While I have a head, I cannot ever talk. You will often see me at the end of the day, and if you need another one, a hefty price you will pay. Who am I?

105 – If you look in my face, you will see someone. However, if you look at my back, you will see no one. Who am I?

106 – While I am feather, I am not a bird, although I have a mobile nest. I can quickly fly, and after I fly, I will also stop and rest. Who am I?

107 – I am a slayer of your regrets, both old and new. While I am sought by many, I am found by very few. Who am I?

108 – I have a blade, and it is jaggedly cut, and I will help

keep your doors shut. I go into the darkness, and I wear a ring. While one of me is quiet, if you have many we will sing. Who am I?

109 – Everyone has me. Those who have the least of me are not aware that they have me. Those who have the most of me, wish they had less of me. But, no one wants to have too little of me or none at all. Who am I?

110 – While I cannot be touched, I can be felt. I cannot be opened, but you can go into me. If you seek me, you will find me under something, yet I can move from place to place. Who am I?

111 – I can make people crazy, and I will shine on you when you retire. I can move water without even a touch, and the colors I turn can cause you ire. Who am I?

112 – I grow from the soil, and live in a scented bed. If you ignore me, I will wither. Use me to apologize or show your love, but remember I need rain from up above. Who am I?

113 – I function like a witch's brew, and I can make people do things they don't want to. At the sound of my voice, you will not have a choice. You have to do what is requested of you. Who am I?

114 – While I see much, I change but little. I am firm and powerful, and I can rip apart a mounting. Yet, the wind can move me. I am often wasted, and sometimes valued. I often stand for life and give life to others. Who am I?

115 – I can easily be given away, but few people want to

take me. People who are older often give me to the young. Sometimes I am true, but I often have a sting. Who am I?

Easy Brain Teaser Answers:

1 – I am the word "Noon"
2 – I am a joke
3 – I am a weapon
4 – I am a daughter
5 – I am a mailman
6 – I am the letter "I"
7 – I am paper
8 – I am a priest
9 – I am ice
10 – I am today
11 – I am curiosity
12 – I am silence
13 – I am a candle
14 – I am a nut
15 – I am a sidewalk
16 – I am a stream
17 – I am a speaker
18 – I am a balloon
19 – I am a diary
20 – I am an optimist
21 – I am a clown
22 – I am cupid
23 – I am an elephant
24 – I am a baseball player
25 – I am a painting
26 – I am peace
27 – I am imagination
28 – I am purple
29 – I am a sloth
30 – I am Christopher Columbus

31 – I am a dentist
32 – I am death

Moderately Hard Brain Teaser Answers:
33 – I am the letter "N"
34 – I am fear
35 – I am an eraser
36 – I am fire
37 – I am soil
38 – I am the wind
39 – I am the game of Chess
40 – I am the King of Spades
41 – I am a firework
42 – I am a television
43 – I am a cannibal
44 – I am a sword
45 – I am hair
46 – I am Santa Claus
47 – I am a teacher
48 – I am the president
49 – I am a comb
50 – I am a hurricane
51 – I am a traffic signal
52 – A am the conductor
53 – I am a teacher
54 – I am your reflection in a mirror
55 – I am freedom
56 – I am a cavity
57 – I am the letter "L"
58 – I am the moon
59 – I am time
60 – I am purple
61 – I am your voice
62 – I am your breath
63 – I am a glove
64 – I am the word "Smiles" (there is a mile between each "S")
65 – I am fire
66 – I am a shadow

67 – I am a doughnut
68 – I am wine
69 – I am a secret
70 – I am darkness
71 – I am a telephone book
72 – I am an onion
73 – I am a towel
74 – I am lunch
75 – I am a snake
76 – I am a chair
77 – I am a milk truck
78 – I am the number 1
79 – I am the stars
80 – I am an envelope
81 – I am a steel chain
82 – I am a stapler
83 – I am a light switch
84 – I am oil
85 – I am a baby
86 – I am the horizon
87 – I am an anchor
88 – I am a promise

Difficult Brain Teaser Answers:

89 – I am a pencil
90 – I am a boat
91 – I am a tornado
92 – I am a doctor
93 – I am the moon
94 – I am the number "12"
95 – I am a bell
96 – am the word "Begins"
97 – I am the truth
98 – I am a sack
99 – I am risk
100 – I am chalk
101 – I am distance
102 – I am bread

103 – I am a flag
104 – I am a bed
105 – I am a mirror
106 – I am an arrow
107 – I am redemption
108 – I am a key
109 – I am age
110 – I am shade
111 – I am the moon
112 – I am a flower
113 – I am the word "please"
114 – I am a tree
115 – I am advice

65 Best Tongue Twisters for Kids

So What's so Good about Tongue Twisters

They can be so much fun especially when you are with a bunch of friends.

Tongue twisters are a real challenge to say for any kid. They use similar sounding syllables, words and sounds repetitively, making it easy for anyone to trip over the words. While tongue twisters for kids can be a whole lot of fun, they also have many practical benefits to offer.

First, tongue twisters for kids can help children to begin speaking clearly. It teaches proper diction of words, since words that have repetitive sounds are difficult to say correctly without good diction. Children learn to speak more clearly when practicing with tongue twisters.

Sometimes it's hard to find good tongue twisters for your children to use. We made it easier by offering you a nice selection of tongue twisters. You'll find easy ones for younger kids, medium difficulty options and difficult tongue twisters that will challenge older kids and even adults. Let your kids have some fun with these tongue twisters as they work to improve their speech and diction at the same time.

So let's try some now!

Easy Tongue Twisters

WARNING
These Tongue Twisters are Clean, But a stumbling
tongue may spill some words not intended.

.

Rubber baby buggy bumpers

.

.

Six slippery snails slowly sliding

.

.

A big box of big biscuits

.

.

Poor Pierre picked purple posies

.

Mad bunny, bad money

Unique New York

The sixth sick sheik's sheep

Fat free fruity float

Twelve tiny twins twirled twelve tiny twigs

Smelly shoes and socks

A big black bug bit a beetle

The tutor tooted the flute

Our oars are of oak

Betty better bring the butter

Baby blue bug baby black bug

Toy boat, toy boat, toy boat

The black bugs blood

Cheap sheep soup, sheep soup

Paint purple pebbles pink,
paint purple pebbles pink

Handsome Samson,
Handsome Samson,
Handsome Samson.

Rooty tooty fruity,
rooty tooty fruit,
rooty tooty fruity

Angie and Annie ate all eight apples

The black bear bit a big black bug

Burglar burgles burgers,
burglar burgles burgers

Snakes silently slither,
silently snakes slither

Funny tummy,
tummy funny,
funny tummy

There's a soldier sitting on your shoulder

Double bubble bubble gum

Greek green grapes grow slow

Nine night nurses nurse nicely

Another benefit of tongue twisters for kids is that they can be used to treat speech problems. Children that have a difficult time saying certain sounds or those struggling with a lisp can benefit from using tongue twisters. Using tongue twisters even helps moms learn letter sounds correctly and word out a child's mouth muscles so they are better able to use more complicated letter sounds.

Medium Difficulty Tongue Twisters

These medium difficulty tongue twisters are great for kids age 10-11 or those who have mastered the easier tongue twisters.

.

Papa wants a proper cup
of coffee in a copper coffee cup

.

.

Crisp crusts crunchily crackle

.

.

The rain in Spain falls mainly on the plain
(from "My Fair Lady")

.

.

Who washes Washington's white woolen underwear

.

.

She sells she shells at the sea shore

.

.

A good cook could cook good

.

.

Lily loves lapping lemonade

Irish wrist watch,
Irish wrist watch,
Irish wrist watch

Sally sang seven slow sad songs slowly

Speedy Sammy the spider
spun six spiderwebs Sunday

A bit of butter Betty bought

Many monsters
munch monster mush

Frenchy fried
flying fish flesh

Freddy found forty-four
furry fun Furbys

We'll weather whether
the weather be fine
or whether it be hot

Yellow butter,
red jelly,
purple jam,
brown bread

Sammy sadly sold Sally's
shoes to a silly skunk

The big busy
buzzing bumble bee
bit Betty

Bitty Bobby bought a ball and bat

To use tongue twisters to their full potential, you'll want to start with easy tongue twisters. Allow them to say it slowly at first as they learn the phrase and the correct sounds. As they become more familiar with the tongue twister, then they can focus on using more speed when saying them. After you become proficient with simple tongue twisters, then you can move on to those that are a bit harder.

Difficult Tongue Twisters

Let your older children try these tongue twisters or have fun trying them yourself.

.

Theophilus Thistle
the unsuccessful thistle sifter
thrust three thistles
through the thick of his thumb

.

.

Peter Piper picked a peck of pickled peppers,
if Peter Piper picked a peck of pickled peppers,
where's the peck of pickled peppers Peter Piper picked.

.

.

Susie sat in a shiny shoe shine shop,
she sits and she shines
and she shines and she sits

.

.

Fuzzy Wuzzy was a bear,
Fuzzy Wuzzy had no hair,
Fuzzy Wuzzy wasn't very fussy, was he?

.

.

How much wood
would a woodchuck chuck
if a woodchuck could chuck wood?
A woodchuck could chuck all the wood
he could if a woodchuck could chuck wood

.

The small skunk sat on a small stump
and on the stump the skunk thunk
and thunk on his stump

You know you need unique New York

Purple princes
and pink princesses
prance playfully around a parade

I thought I had a thought
but the thought wasn't the thought
that I thought I thought

Terry tickled Timmy's ticklish tummy,
when Terry tickled Timmy's ticklish tummy,
Timmy tickled Terry's tummy too

The brave brisk brigadiers
brandished bright blades and
bludgeons with bad balance

How many bright blue berries
could a bear berry carrier carry
if the bear berry carrier
could carry bright blue berries.

Betty bought a box of baking powder
to bake a batch of biscuits.
Betty places the biscuits in the basket
and took the biscuits in the basket to the bakery

.

.

Picky prickly people
pick Peter Pan peanut butter
because it's the peanut butter
that the picky prickly people pick

.

.

Sally sells her shells at the sea shore,
but if she sells her sea shells at the sea shore,
where are the sea shells Sally likes to sell

.

.

Bitty Bobby bought a bat and ball,
then Bobby use the bat
to bang the ball against the wall.

.

ABOUT THE AUTHOR

Peter MacDonald loves a good laugh, especially ones he can share with his children. He is committed to creating good clean fun in His series of joke books, "Best Joke Books For Kids". Peter is an Aussie with a good sense of Humor and he enjoys the good things in life, especially his church and family.

Made in the USA
Coppell, TX
09 April 2020

19223753R00095